Restoring

Our

Earth

Laurence Pri

ENSLOW PUBLISHERS, INC.

Bloy St. & Ramsey Ave.	P.O. Box 38
Box 777	Aldershot
Hillside, N.J. 07205	Hants GU12 6BP
U.S.A.	U.K.

Library of Congress Cataloging in Publication Data

Pringle, Laurence P.
 Restoring our earth

 Bibliography: p.
 Includes index.
 Summary: Discusses the ecological restoration of prairies, marshes, forests, rivers, and other damaged environments of North America.
  1. Nature conservation. 2. Reclamation of land. 3. Environmental protection. 4. Landscape protection. [1. Environmental protection] I. Title.
 QH75.P755 1987 333.7'2 87-615
 ISBN 0-89490-143-5

Printed in the United States of America
10 9 8 7 6 5 4 3 2 1

Illustration Credits

Sven Bjørk, p. 49; Edgar Garbisch, Jr., Environmental Concern, Inc., pp. 9, 10, 12; Fermi Accelerator Laboratory, pp. 20, 22; Jon Giffen, p. 36; Linda Golder, p. 43 (bottom); Eugene Kridler, p. 35; National Park Service, photo by Robert Belous, p. 32; National Park Service, photo by Bruce Kilgore, p. 29; New York State Department of Environmental Conservation, photo by John Goerg, p. 47; Office of Surface Mining, U.S. Department of the Interior, p. 50; Laurence Pringle, pp. 8, 27, 30, 34, 48, 58; Francis Smith, pp. 4, 43 (top & middle); South Florida Water Management District, photo by Patrick W. Partington, p. 40; South Florida Water Management District, p. 44; Tennessee Valley Authority, pp. 51, 53, 54, 56; Tiburon Center for Environmental Studies, cover, p. 15; U.S. Army Corps of Engineers, p. 13; University of Wisconsin Arboretum, photo by Betsy Doehlert, p. 17; University of Wisconsin Arboretum, photo by Theodore Sperry, pp. 19, 25.

Contents

A restored section of the Quashnet River on Cape Cod, Massachusetts.

CHAPTER ONE

Reassembling Nature

In San Francisco Bay and Chesapeake Bay, men and women slog through deep mud to plant cordgrasses and create new marshes. In the Midwest, people search in old cemeteries for patches of native prairie plants and collect some of their seeds for propagation. In Florida, a straightened river may be restored to its old meandering channel.

All over North America people are working to restore marshes, prairies, rangelands, forests, lakes, rivers, and other damaged environments. A new scientific field, ecological restoration, is emerging. As defined by John Berger in his book *Restoring the Earth,* "Restoration is an effort to imitate nature in all its artistry and complexity by taking a degraded system and making it more diverse and productive."

Restoration is *not* reclamation. A developer may boast of "reclaiming" land when he fills or drains a marsh in order to create dry land for homesites. Strip-mined land may be said to be reclaimed when it is covered with a growth of grasses, probably species from Europe or Asia rather than plants native to the area. The land may be reclaimed, but it isn't restored.

Given time, a disturbed piece of land or body of water will often restore itself to some extent. In Great Britain, a beautiful natural area called the Norfolk Broads was discovered to be a former peat-industry site. Over four centuries, until about the year 1500, peat was dug from the area,

5

leaving several steep-walled basins that eventually filled with water. No doubt it was an ugly landscape when first abandoned. Today the area is a complex of shallow lakes, marshes, and forests, rich with wildlife, and has been declared a nature reserve.

A weedy city lot can also become a forest if undisturbed for a few decades, although it will lack many plants and animals that are natives of that region. Restoration ecologists seek to influence this process of change and to speed it up. They encourage and also reintroduce plants and animals that are native to an area. They try to wipe out and keep out organisms from other regions that are not native.

In a sense, a damaged piece of land or body of water is like a fine watch that someone blithely took apart and cast aside. The restoration challenge: to reassemble the parts and make the complex device work again. (Reclamation of the parts would produce something useful but not the same intricate timepiece.) Restoration often calls for knowledge of ecology, botany, zoology, agriculture, engineering, and agronomy, or soils science. It has been called the "acid test of ecological understanding," because it asks humans, with their imperfect knowledge, to imitate nature.

Restoration of lands and waters also gives ecologists an opportunity to test ideas, to reassemble an environment piece by piece, and to observe the effects. This basic research could lead to a new understanding of how living and nonliving things depend on one another.

No less important are the immediate tangible results of restoration—formerly degraded places made into prairies, marshes, forests, and other natural places with their diverse plant-animal communities. As these healed wounds delight our senses, they remind us that we have the ability to refashion our landscape in positive as well as negative ways.

CHAPTER TWO

Marsh Builders

"The ribbon of green marshes, part solid land, part mobile water, has a definite but elusive border, now hidden, now exposed, as the tides of the Atlantic fluctuate. . . . The marsh reaches as far inland as the tides can creep and as far into the sea as marsh plants can find a roothold and live in saline waters."

John and Mildred Teal
Life and Death of the Salt Marsh

Of all marshes, swamps, and other wetlands, saltwater marshes produce the most living matter. These wet meadows are washed daily by tides. Outgoing tides carry bits of dead grass and other edible organic matter into the deeper waters of a bay—food for oysters and other shellfish. Incoming tides allow fish, crabs, and squid to reach the low parts of the marsh. Salt marshes serve as feeding grounds, spawning beds, and nurseries for marine fish and crustaceans. Destruction of salt marshes spells the end of many kinds of seafood valued by humans.

People have so far wiped out about half of the ribbon of green marshes that once flourished along the coastal United States. California, for example, once had 381,000 acres of coastal wetlands; now it has about 105,000 acres. Former salt marshes are now covered by cities, housing tracts, airports, landfills, or simply by soil washed off the land and carried by rivers into bays and lagoons. The human impact includes diking and draining marshes, and changing the amount and content of fresh water flowing into bays and other estuaries.

Egrets find refuge and food in salt marshes along the New Jersey shore. Atlantic City is in the background.

In the 1960s increasing numbers of people learned to appreciate the value of salt marshes and to protect them. One book, published in 1969, played a role in changing public attitudes toward salt marshes. *Life and Death of the Salt Marsh*, by John and Mildred Teal, eloquently explained that salt marshes are one of nature's great gifts, a bounty being squandered by humanity.

Sometimes a person's life is changed by a book. *Life and Death of the Salt Marsh* had a great effect on a man named Edgar Garbisch, Jr. In 1970 Garbisch took a temporary leave from the University of Minnesota, where he was a successful research chemist and teacher. He was looking for work with more tangible results. Although Garbisch had spent boyhood summers beside Chesapeake Bay, he had never paid much attention to its salt marshes. Now, living by the bay again at age thirty-seven, he began to learn about the marshes, their value, and their destruction by people.

Garbisch felt we could do more than just protect the marshes that remained. There were opportunities to restore marshes in places where they had been damaged and to create marshes where they had never existed. In fact, the authors of *Life and Death of the Salt Marsh* had written: "There seems to be no reason why the construction of new marshland would be an impossibility. . . . It might be possible to get a new marsh well established within only a few years if it were adequately planted. We know of no case in which this has been tried."

Ed Garbisch was fascinated. After further study and success with a small-scale planting of marsh grasses, he resigned from his university job. He became a marsh builder.

At first he believed a staff of scientists would be needed to learn how to restore salt marshes. But most of the problems that arose did not require long study or complex research. They were mainly technical problems, such as finding or adapting machinery or equipment for the peculiar job of marsh-building. When planting grass seedlings by hand, for example, workers sometimes needed to wear plastic-covered snowshoes to keep from sinking deep into the gooey marsh mud.

Modified snowshoes were tried for a time but are no longer used by crew members when they plant seedlings by hand.

In 1972 Garbisch created a nonprofit organization, Environmental Concern, Inc., with headquarters in the fishing village of St. Michaels, Maryland, on the eastern shore of Chesapeake Bay. That spring he also began the first known full-scale attempt to create a salt marsh. The site was Hambleton Island, a mile from St. Michaels. In the mid-1800s the island had been 55 acres in size, but waves and currents had eroded about half of it away. Erosion had also cut the uninhabited island in two.

To halt erosion, Garbisch decided to plant a new marsh in the channel that bisected the island. The channel was too deep for marsh grasses to grow, so the first step was to partly fill it with sand. Three hundred bargeloads of sand were needed to raise the channel bottom to the desired level. Then Ed Garbisch and his work crew, along with friends and volunteers began to hand-transplant a quarter million seedlings of marsh grasses. The job took five months to complete. The grasses took hold and began to flourish. Then they were flattened by the high winds and waves of a hurricane. For a few days the situation looked grim, but the grasses recovered. The new Hambleton Island marsh grew thick and tall, slowing erosion and attracting animal life both above and below water.

Salt marshes can be established by scattering cordgrass seeds from a moving airboat, then dragging the area to cover them with mud.

The success of this first human-made marsh led to new opportunities. Environmental Concern each year restores or creates dozens of marshes for communities, government agencies, corporations, and private landowners. Most of the projects are located along the East Coast, but Environmental Concern has also restored freshwater marshes as far inland as Ohio.

To build a marsh one needs native marsh plants—duck potato, arrow arum, and pickerelweed for freshwater sites, and the two species of cordgrass that dominate eastern salt-water marshes. Cordgrasses have the scientific name *Spartina,* from the Greek word for cord, because people used to twist similar grasses into thin ropes. One species of cordgrass, *Spartina alterniflora,* grows up to 10 feet high in low marsh areas that are flooded twice daily by tides. The other common eastern species, *Spartina patens,* sometimes called salt hay, grows about 2 feet tall in marsh areas that are inundated by only the highest tides.

Each year Ed Garbisch grows as many as a half million *Spartina* seedlings in a wetland nursery. These plants are raised from seeds, and many salt marshes are restored by direct planting of seeds. So in early autumn each year the staff of Environmental Concern harvests about 500 gallons of *Spartina* seeds from existing marshes.

Compared with the challenge of restoring a forest, prairie, or other land ecosystem, salt marsh restoration is relatively easy. Once *Spartina* grasses are established, other saltwater organisms are carried in by the tides. Within five years cordgrasses lay down a peatlike layer of dead leaves and stems. Soon it is hard to tell a new marsh from one that has existed for scores of years.

Nevertheless, getting a new marsh off to a good start can be difficult. The grade, or height of land in relation to the tides, is critical for cordgrasses. Marsh plants fail to survive if the grade is off by a few inches. Establishing a favorable grade at a site requires knowledge of the tides, surveying, and careful work with earth-moving equipment. Even with an ideal grade, however, cordgrasses fail to survive if the land rises too steeply. A steep slope invites erosion; the incline toward higher ground must be very gentle to minimize wave impact. Even then waves may wash away newly planted *Spartina.* Temporary baffles, or low stone walls, may be needed to tame the waves. Given a few months' protection, *Spartina* seedlings grow into a thick mat of soil-trapping vegetation.

One benefit of salt marshes, whether natural or planted by people, is that they control erosion. Environmental Concern is frequently asked by landowners to stop shoreline erosion. The conventional but expensive remedy is to line the shore with a wall of stones. At many sites Environmental Concern established a 25-foot-wide strip of wave-taming marsh for one tenth the cost of a stone barrier. The lush ribbon of green, more attractive than stones, is also a habitat for fish, crustaceans, and other wildlife.

The top photo shows an eroding shoreline where cordgrasses were planted by Environmental Concern. The bottom photo shows the same shore three months later.

Environmental Concern is often hired to repair or replace marshes that have been harmed by construction or draining. Usually a utility or corporation is allowed by government to destroy some marsh only on the condition that an equal or greater area of marsh is created elsewhere. (A larger area is usually demanded, on the assumption that human-made marsh does not match the value of the original wetland.) This tradeoff is called mitigation, and mitigation projects make up 60 percent of Environmental Concern's work.

In the mid-1970s, the U.S. Army Corps of Engineers began an effort to establish marshes and other natural habitats on the mud and silt dredged from harbors and shipping channels. Tides and currents continually carry silt into these channels, and nationwide the Corps of Engineers dredges up more than 350 million cubic yards a year. The bottom muck is commonly dumped back into the water, away from the channel, where it may kill bottom-dwelling shellfish and may also be gradually swept back into the channel. Hauling the dredged material to land is costly, and few landowners want the stuff anyway. In Chesapeake Bay the Corps of Engineers has hired Ed Garbisch and his staff to make salt marshes on dredged material.

Mud and silt dredged from a channel is dumped onto a barge. Disposal of this dredged material is a big problem.

After successfully establishing salt marshes up to 10 acres in size on dredged sediments, in 1982 Environmental Concern tackled the largest project of this kind. The corps dredged a channel near Barren Island in Chesapeake Bay, and Ed Garbisch had the 180,000 cubic yards of sediments deposited in a huge, nearly flat pile near the island. Garbisch directed the dumping of the silt and mud so that about 27 acres of land were exposed at low tide. The new island sloped very gently up toward a crown that was 27 inches above normal high spring tides, an elevation that was needed for nesting by least terns, an endangered species whose production the corps wanted to encourage.

The following spring Environmental Concern's work crews scattered *Spartina* seeds and planted *Spartina* seedlings on 25 acres of the island. The plants began to grow, to trap silt, and to stabilize the dredged material. By midsummer of 1982 the new island's crown was adorned with a large nesting colony of least terns.

Although Ed Garbisch is considered the master marsh builder on the eastern seaboard, marsh restoration efforts are being made all along the U.S. coast. The basic operating principles remain the same, but may involve the use of different native plants. Near Tampa, Florida, for example, red mangroves were planted with cordgrasses along 10 miles of shoreline to help stabilize the soil in front of a housing development.

In Southern California, the cordgrass *Spartina foliosa* dominates the lowest areas of salt marshes, while pickleweed is most common in the middle and high marshes. Such plants as saltwort and arrow grass are also abundant in the middle marsh elevations. As part of their effort to make salt marshes as natural as possible, ecologists try to exclude or discourage exotic plants. In Southern California these include the white mangrove from New Zealand and sickle grass from Europe.

Marsh grasses being planted at low tide in southern San Francisco Bay.

The simplest and least expensive way to restore a marsh calls for no planting but simply returning tidal flows to areas that were drained or somehow blocked from the ocean's tides. In 1980, full tidal flow was restored to Pine Creek Marsh in Fairfield, Connecticut. Upland plants that could not tolerate salt water disappeared, and the area was quickly colonized by salt-marsh plants.

Ecologists recognize that they cannot restore a salt marsh to conditions that existed before Europeans settled in North America. We don't even know what salt marshes were like then; old maps reveal only their locations, not detailed accounts of their plant-animal communities. Also, even without the impact of humans, marshes have been altered by floods, droughts, hurricanes, and other natural calamities. By reversing the human damage whenever possible and by replacing native plants and animals that have been lost, marsh builders aim to create the most natural coastal wetlands possible today.

CHAPTER THREE

Sowing Grasslands

"What a thousand acres of Silphiums [compass plants] looked like when they tickled the bellies of the buffalo is a question never again to be answered, and perhaps not even asked."

Aldo Leopold
A Sand County Almanac

On a recent spring day, clouds of gray smoke rose high above the arboretum of the University of Wisconsin at Madison. Anyone who rushed to the scene of the fire found part of the 60-acre Curtis Prairie ablaze and the rest already looking like a blackened wasteland. Within a few minutes fire had scorched the entire prairie—a grassland that ecologists had restored over a period of more than fifty years.

Far from a tragedy, the fire had been deliberately set for the benefit of the prairie's plant-animal community. Fire kills invading weeds, shrubs, and trees but stimulates the growth of native grasses and other deep-rooted prairie plants. Anyone who seeks to restore or maintain a prairie tries to include regular controlled fires.

In pre-Colonial times, only rain or a large river halted the periodic fires that swept over vast areas of the original 700,000,000 acres of North American prairie. This sea of grass covered the middle third of the United States and parts of southern Alberta, Saskatchewan, and Manitoba, Canada. Other types of prairies grew in the Southwest, in arid eastern Oregon and Washington, and even on New York's Long Island.

Fire was a natural force in wild prairies, and ecologists use controlled fires to maintain and improve restored grasslands.

Tallgrass prairie, dominated by plants up to 10 feet high, grew where annual rainfall was 35 inches or more. As explorers and settlers headed west into more arid climates, the tall grasses gave way to medium and short grasses.

With the settlers came livestock, fences, and steel "sodbusting" plows. Wheat and corn replaced Indian grass, big bluestem, and compass plant in the rich prairie soil. The original prairie disappeared fast. Many remnants were protected from fire, and so were invaded by weeds and trees.

Some people mourned the loss of the grassland sea and its diverse wildlife. One such person was Aldo Leopold, an ecologist-philosopher whose wisdom about the relationship between humans and nature is part of the foundation on which the environmental movement is based. In 1934 Leopold and other biologists at the University of Wisconsin decided to establish an arboretum—usually a collection of living "specimen" plants, especially trees. The university bought nearly 2 square miles of forest, pasture, and cornfields just west of Madison. Little patches of prairie remained, but most of the original prairie had become oak forest; then most of that had been logged and grazed by livestock. It was a fine example of ecologically degraded Wisconsin land.

Speaking at the arboretum dedication in 1934, Leopold announced a unique goal: Rather than a collection of plants, the arboretum was to be a collection of natural plant-animal communities. "Our goal in a nutshell," he said, "is to recon-struct a sample of original Wisconsin—a sample of what Dane County looked like when our ancestors arrived here during the 1840s."

Today the arboretum is made up of more than thirty kinds of plant-animal communities, representing all of the major ecological communities of Wisconsin. They include several types of forest, including red pine, white pine, and maple, and two large prairies. Of all these ecosystems, the prairie restorations have been the most successful.

Ecologist Theodore Sperry was given the novel task of re-storing a prairie in the spring of 1936. Sperry recalls that, "Neither I nor, so far as I have learned, anyone else ever attempted to recreate a native prairie from an old field which still contained the stubble of old corn stalks in its cover of ragweed and quack grass."

Fortunately, Sperry had the aid of Civilian Conservation Corps workers. The Civilian Conservation Corps was an agency of the federal government that provided outdoor work for many thousands of young men who were unemployed at that time. With the help of some of these men, Sperry began to transplant sod from existing prairie remnants. Although some of these prairie patches were in the path of develop-ment, robbing one natural community in order to restore an-other is frowned upon by today's restorationists. Different plant species were set in separate, numbered plots. When Sperry left the arboretum in 1941, almost 30 tons of prairie sod had been brought in, with forty-six species of prairie plants covering about 60 acres in a crazy-quilt pattern.

Despite this strong start, Sperry said that the prairie resto-ration would take a thousand years. He had been particularly troubled by alien weeds that competed with native plants. Be-fore leaving he began to experiment with a new and then con-troversial method of weed control—fire.

Workers of the Civilian Conservation Corps dug up many tons of prairie sod for replanting at the University of Wisconsin Arboretum.

Botanist John Curtis soon began to use and study prairie fire in a systematic way, burning test plots every year or every other year, in March, May, or October. He found that fire clearly discouraged alien weeds without harming native plants. Since 1933 the whole 60-acre prairie—now named for Curtis—has been burned regularly.

Eventually the arboretum acquired a second tract of land and began restoring part of it to prairie. Through the years a great variety of prairie plants has been added to the two prairies. Although patches of exotic weeds still remain, the Curtis Prairie may now have a greater diversity of native plants than existed in many original prairies. To a restoration ecologist, having a greater than normal variety of native plants or less variety than normal is the same—an unnatural situation.

The pioneering restoration effort at Curtis Prairie drew visitors to the project and inspired scores of similar restoration attempts. Botanical gardens, universities, parks, and even elementary and high schools have established prairies to give the public a glimpse of once-vast grasslands. Some rival or excede the Curtis Prairie in size; many are small and can be kept weed-free by hand. A 10-acre prairie restoration project at the University of Minnesota Arboretum is funded in part by Minnesota's highway department, which is investigating the use of native grassland plants along roadways. Besides adding beauty to highway rights-of-way, prairie plants may reduce maintenance costs of highway departments.

The largest prairie restoration in the United States is under way about 30 miles west of Chicago on property owned by the U.S. Department of Energy. This is the site of the Fermi Accelerator Laboratory (Fermilab), where research on high-energy physics goes on. The laboratory's proton accelerator itself is an underground circular tunnel, 3.6 miles in circumference. Within that circle lie 650 acres of land. In 1972, when Fermilab was under construction, officials sought some land-scaping advice from the nearby Morton Arboretum, where a fine 25-acre prairie had been created. Three ecologists decided to persuade Fermilab administrators to create a huge prairie within the accelerator circle. After all, this *was* Illinois, "the prairie state." In 1974 the lab granted permission.

An aerial view of the Fermilab circle. It encloses 650 acres of land, of which about 460 acres are restored to prairie.

Within the accelerator ring lay some small lakes, marshes, patches of native bur-oak forest, and about 460 acres of fallow farmland covered with such exotic plants as quack grass and

Hungarian brome. Ecologists found fewer than a dozen species of native prairie plants. The restoration task seemed enormous.

They started small, plowing and disking 8 acres of farmland. In the fall of 1974, nearly a hundred volunteers, mostly Fermilab employees, fanned out in a 50-mile radius of the site, searching for some seventy species of native prairie plants. Old cemeteries and railroad rights-of-way were desirable hunting places. Some of the long, narrow strips of land along railroads were fenced off before the original prairies were plowed. Aldo Leopold wrote, "The outstanding conservator of the prairie flora, ironically enough, knows little and cares less about such frivolities: it is the railroad with its fenced right-of-way."

The volunteers collected about 400 pounds of clean seeds, which were sown in June 1975. The immediate results were not encouraging. Despite the spring disking of the soil, intended to kill weeds, the weeds sprang up all over. As ecologist Robert Betz of Northeastern Illinois University recalls, "The weeds grabbed that land, and we had ragweed towering over the land; we had lamb's quarters; we had daisies; we had thistles; we had everything."

Everything, it appeared, except native plants. Leading a tour of the area, Betz had to get down on his hands and knees to find little sprigs of prairie plants. But Betz knew that these plants establish sizable root systems before showing much aboveground growth. Sure enough, within three years the grass grew tall and thick. Alien weeds were losing ground. By the spring of the fourth year ecologists added fire as an ally, and the native plants continued to gain.

Each year another patch of land was plowed, disked, and planted. Seeds were spread by a modified highway salt-spreader attached to the back of a vehicle with large balloonlike tires, which do not leave noticeable tracks. Thirty acres of new prairie were added in 1979. By that time the project workers no longer had to search beyond Fermilab for their seeds. Using a farm combine, they harvested many thousands of pounds of seeds from the Fermilab prairie itself. These seeds were later mixed with seeds collected from other areas in order to increase the diversity of the plant community.

A combine harvester collects seeds from native plants established at Fermilab; the seeds are used to restore prairie to new areas.

By the summer of 1985 all large tracts of potential prairie had been planted, and the restoration work extended beyond the accelerator ring to other Fermilab land. It could eventually encompass another 500 acres.

The world's largest restored prairie is a great success, but the work is far from complete. Some Hungarian brome and other exotic weeds persist; the prairie still lacks some native plants and animals. Certain native plants do not propagate well by direct seeding. They include leadplant, blue joint grass, and marsh blazing star. These plants were raised in a nursery, and then transplanted as seedlings in May before the established plants begin to grow.

Sandhill cranes and trumpeter swans, once natives of the Illinois prairie, have been introduced to the Fermilab grounds, although they are held captive. Project ecologists hope that migratory flocks of these species can eventually be established. They also plan to reintroduce smaller creatures, such as Franklin's ground squirrel, the yellow-winged grasshopper, and prairie katydids—all creatures that once inhabited the area.

Bringing back native animals is a goal of many restoration projects. The size of a prairie restoration may determine whether a population of a native animal can survive. Without space of a minimum critical size the population will fail. For the grasshopper sparrow, the minimum critical size is about 12 acres; for Henslow's sparrow, 100 acres; for the upland sandpiper, 300 acres. If a single prairie lacks the minimum space, a cluster of smaller prairies may meet the needs of an animal population.

Ecologists are also concerned about animals already existing in restored prairies. There are, for example, flightless insects that spend the winter aboveground as eggs or nymphs. They might not survive if an entire small prairie is burned in the spring. Some restored prairies are homes for threatened or endangered species of butterflies or flowers. The survival of these populations may depend on choosing the right time to set a prairie fire.

Some of the most difficult plants to restore are forbs—herbs that grow among the grasses. Many forbs were common or dominant plants in prairies but are rare or absent on restored sites. Forbs include compass plant, leadplant, purple coneflower, prairie dock, yellow baptisia, wild quinine, and rough blazing star. As some of their names suggest, forbs produce the flowers that carpet prairies from May to October. Ecologists usually raise forbs from seeds, then transplant seedlings into partly restored prairie areas to increase their beauty and diversity.

Prairie ecologists have learned that the restoration process involves not only ridding a site of alien plants but also taking steps to keep them out. Some commercial nurseries that sell native prairie grasses and forbs also sell exotic clovers, grasses, and Eurasian weeds. Prairie grasses are also promoted without regard for their place of origin in North America. Ecologists warn against mixing native species from, say, shortgrass prairie and tallgrass prairie. They urge that seeds be collected from sources as close as possible to the restoration site in order to help make the plant community more authentic.

Ecologists are now paying more attention to the "invisible prairie"—the below-ground part of a plant-animal community. In a shortgrass prairie there may be twice as much living material below ground as there is above. The hidden portion consists of plant roots and rhizomes, soil-dwelling insects, worms, small mammals, and microorganisms.

The root of a compass plant, ready for transplanting. The "invisible prairie" includes the large root systems of native plants and the mycorrhizae fungi associated with them.

Especially important are fungi called mycorrhizae, which grow on or within plant roots and reach beyond the roots into the soil, absorbing nutrients that are returned to the plant. Mycorrhizae also seem to help plants survive drought. Although mycorrhizae are not well understood, ecologists know that they play a key role in the establishment and survival of many plants.

Thus, in order to truly restore prairies, ecologists find themselves studying and reintroducing mycorrhizae fungi, earthworms, ants, and other underground natives.

CHAPTER FOUR

Healing Woodlands

"So, when we experiment in planting forests we find
ourselves at last doing as Nature does. Would it not be
well to consult with Nature in the outset? for she is the
most extensive and experienced planter of us all. . . ."

Henry David Thoreau
The Succession of Forest Trees

For countless years people have felled trees to clear land for
agriculture and homesites, for lumber, fuel, wood pulp (used
to make paper), and bark (used to tan leather). North American forests seemed inexhaustible, but by 1750 eastern cities
suffered from wood shortages—which, incidentally, led to the
invention of more efficient wood stoves. Early in the twentieth century, people still resisted the idea of setting aside forest reserves. "The plow will follow the ax" was conventional
wisdom; therefore a devastated forest was considered a step
toward progress. Some forests were spared, however, and
professional foresters began to direct tree-planting programs.

Demand for forest products has grown with the earth's
population. Existing forests must be carefully managed, and
new forests must be planted. The need for reforestation has
never been greater, especially in such nations as India and
China, where loss of woodlands causes severe erosion and
devastating floods. A forest serves as a sort of natural sponge,
soaking up rainwater and releasing it gradually into streams.

In 1980 only 12.7 percent of China was forested. This rep-
resents less than a third of an acre per person; the world aver-
age is about 2.5 acres of woodland per person. In 1982 the

Chinese government launched a campaign to reforest more than 270,000 square miles of land.

Abroad and in the United States, most reforestation projects do not aim to recreate a natural forest community with a rich variety of native life. Indeed, the goal is often the opposite: to establish a forest dominated by a single species, a monoculture forest. An exotic species of fast-growing coniferous (evergreen) tree may be planted in rows where a forest of mixed deciduous trees once stood. Tree plantations like this support such a limited plant-animal community that ecologists have called them biological deserts.

There are, however, people working to truly restore forests or to maintain wild woodlands in as natural a condition as possible. In some national parks and forests, especially in the arid West, this includes allowing forest fires to burn. Just as fire was and is beneficial in prairie environments, it is a driving force in the life cycles of many forest plants and animals.

A plantation of a single coniferous tree species offers little diversity to attract and support a variety of animal life.

In pre-Colonial days, periodic fires were common in southeastern forests of longleaf pine and in western forests of ponderosa pine, sequoia, white pine, lodgepole pine, larch, and Douglas fir. Denied fire, forests of these trees do not thrive; they can be protected out of existence. An occasional ground fire burns dead leaves and limbs that have fallen beneath trees. If this material is allowed to accumulate for many years it provides fuel for an intense blaze that can severely damage a forest.

In the United States, the possibility of protecting forests to death was belatedly recognized in the early 1960s. The emphasis has changed from all-out fire suppression to fire management. In numerous western national parks and national forests, areas called natural fire zones or fire management areas have been established. Within these zones, lightning-caused fires are usually allowed to burn.

Every forest fire is unique, with different conditions of terrain, wind, moisture, and the amount, kinds, and distribution of dead leaves and other fuel. Understanding the "behavior" of fires and managing them is no easy task. In 1980 a fire set deliberately in Michigan's Huron National Forest was supposed to burn about 200 acres of jack-pine forest and improve the habitat of the rare Kirtland's warbler. Winds took the fire out of control; it covered 28,000 acres and burned dozens of homes.

Usually fire managers err on the side of caution. In 1985 the United States Forest Service tried to start a fire in a Colorado forest, dropping napalm (jellied gasoline) from a helicopter. Fire failed to start because the woods were too wet that day. Foresters were eventually successful in setting fire to several thousand acres of lodgepole pine and Douglas fir. Their goal was to rejuvenate the woodlands and to open grazing ground for a herd of bighorn sheep.

Fires are sometimes deliberately set by ecologists who seek to return this natural force to western national parks.

Managers of national forests and national parks also face the challenge of convincing the public that fire can be a force for positive change. For decades people have been encouraged to believe that all forest fires are bad. Old ideas die slowly, so part of the task of restoring fire to woodlands is public education.

Forest restorations are under way in many states, in state and county parks, and on lands administered by universities, arboretums, and other institutions. Some restorations are tiny. One in Chicago measures 75 by 100 feet. It was a littered vacant lot when purchased in the early 1970s by Eugene Chesrow, a commodities trader. He planted native trees, shrubs, ferns, and wildflowers. Now owned by the Chicago Audubon Society, the little forest is like an oasis of green in a busy commercial neighborhood. Eugene Chesrow lives beside the forest, waters it in the summertime, and removes beer cans and wine bottles from the forest floor.

In New York City another tiny forest, 45 by 200 feet, was begun in 1978 by artist Alan Sonfist. Called "Time Landscape," it shows three stages of a lower Manhattan forest in pre-Colonial times—first grasses and wildflowers, then saplings, and finally mature trees.

Given enough time, "Time Landscape" will give people in New York City a glimpse of the type of forest that once flourished there.

Projects like these have esthetic and educational value, but are too small to represent a functioning forest ecosystem. Most forest restorations involve a score of acres or more. The largest by far is under way at California's Redwood National Park.

In this park the National Park Service faced an unusual challenge. Of 48,000 acres in the Redwood Creek basin added to the park in 1978, 36,000 had been logged. Soil and tree limbs had been pushed into streams, and rainwater washing down steep slopes and logging roads eroded gullies and carried sediments into Redwood Creek. Furthermore, Congress had excluded the upper two thirds of the basin from the park, and logging there caused more eroded sediments to reach Redwood Creek and its tributaries.

By 1975 the annual erosion rate was more than 8,000 tons per square mile, an estimated eight times greater than the amount before logging. The increased sediment load had filled stream channels, with the result that overflowing water eroded streamside stands of Douglas fir in the upper basin and threatened downstream terraces, where groves of the earth's tallest trees still flourished.

Congress directed the National Park Service to restore areas that had been logged both within and outside the park, and also to reduce damage along Redwood Creek. The park service plan aimed to halt erosion from already-logged slopes and 200 miles of logging roads, and also to review timber-cutting plans for the private lands upstream of the park.

Much of the work involves bulldozers and other heavy equipment, but a lot of hand labor is needed to spread straw mulch and to plant trees and shrubs. The undisturbed portions of the park serve as a model, or reference, for ecologists seeking to restore vegetation to its natural habitat. To protect soil along streamsides, for example, coyote brush is planted on the dry side of the basin, and red alder on the moist side. The park's restoration ecologists have found red alder to be their single most useful plant. This shrub spreads quickly over barren logged areas, stabilizing the soil where Douglas fir and redwoods will eventually stand.

Not all of Redwood National Park is forested. Grasslands occur naturally on the tops of ridges and along the eastern flank of the basin. The two dominant native grasses are California oat grass and wild blue rye, but some exotic species have become common in the region since about 1850. Park ecologists have not tried to eliminate the alien plants. Their research shows, however, that more than 30 percent of the basin's prairies have been taken over by trees since periodic fires were stopped in the mid-1800s. The return of fire would halt the encroaching forest and perhaps suppress exotic grasses too.

Logging abuse of the basin's forests and soils also affected life in Redwood Creek and its tributaries—once spawning sites for trout and salmon. Logging debris and eroded soil choked stream channels, keeping fish from reaching their native breeding areas. Park biologists plan to clear these

At Redwood National Park, workers replant a streamside slope with seedlings of red alder, redwood, and Douglas fir.

A geologist inspects a logged slope that was recontoured by bulldozers and made ready for planting with native shrubs and trees.

A two-year-old Douglas fir is planted on a site that was logged before the national park was established.

obstacles slowly in order to avoid sudden release of dammed-up accumulations of sediments. Deposits of gravel have filled many former pools in the lower 18 miles of Redwood Creek. Even though much less sediment now flows downstream, these deposits prevent the full recovery of fish populations. Perhaps only decades of winter floods will carry away enough sediment so that trout, salmon, and other fish will thrive again in Redwood Creek.

All national parks are supposed to be kept undamaged for the "enjoyment of future generations." Each park has a management plan, but the overall goal is to preserve and protect, not to alter. At Redwood National Park, however, the park service first had to repair massive damage, to heal the land in order to establish a self-sustaining redwood forest ecosystem. Since coastal redwoods can live to two thousand years of age, trees planted in the 1980s won't be mature for many centuries. Commenting on this, William R. Jordan III, editor of *Restoration & Management Notes,* wrote, "Anyone who undertakes a restoration project has to live in an imagined future, and in the case of the redwoods this implies a long view indeed."

National parks are supposed to be "vignettes of primitive America"—natural ecosystems kept as undisturbed as possible. To achieve this, sometimes such native life as wild turkeys and otters are restored to their former habitats; the reintroduction of timber wolves to Yellowstone National Park is being studied. Many state natural resource departments have successfully brought native wildlife back to parks and forest reserves.

Ecologists have found that the presence or absence of native animals can affect plant restoration. In Wisconsin, for example, attempts to restore white cedars in a swamp conifer forest have been thwarted by a white-tailed deer population that winters in the swamp. Cedar is a favorite deer food, and deer-proof fences may be needed to allow white cedars to grow.

At the University of Wisconsin Arboretum, ecologists found that ant populations affect the spread of certain wildflowers in restored forests. Decades ago, wildflowers were planted near trails. Some species have since dispersed throughout the forest. But bloodroot and wild ginger have failed to spread far, although they grow in large patches where they were originally planted. Investigation showed that a nearby natural forest had two hundred times more ants and twice as many ant species as the restored woodlands. Seeds are normally carried off by ants for food. Uneaten seeds sprout and grow, and the plants are dispersed in that way. To help the plants disperse, ecologists may introduce certain ant species to the restored forest.

While encouraging native species, restoration ecologists discourage nonnatives. The National Park Service began to move against alien animals in the 1970s. With the help of a

Ants play a role in the seed dispersal of bloodroot.

private organization called the Fund for Animals, the park service has rid Grand Canyon National Park of burros and is removing them from Death Valley National Monument. The Fund for Animals seeks people who will adopt the burros as pets.

Other alien pests, much more difficult to eradicate, are the feral pigs that live in the forests of Hawaii Volcanoes National Park. No one can give an accurate tally of all the harm done by pigs, since little is known about the native flora and fauna *before* pigs were released centuries ago on all major Hawaiian islands. The effects of pigs were shown dramatically, however, when they were fenced out of a 1,080-square-yard area so that conditions inside could be compared with those outside. After thirteen years the outside area had more exposed soil and roots, a greater number of exotic plant species, and a more abundant growth of exotic grasses and herbs.

Wildlife biologists in Hawaii have studied the behavior of feral pigs in order to learn how to reduce their numbers.

Within the pig-free area there were fewer exposed roots, fewer exotic plants, more native plants, and less exposed soil. The protected area was a sort of pig-free island, somewhat resembling old Hawaii, surrounded by a pig-ravaged landscape.

In the mountainous Hawaiian forest, pigs break open the trunks of fallen tree ferns and eat the starchy interior. By doing so they prevent the tree fern from recovering. Normally a fallen tree fern regenerates, sending a stem upward, which quickly fills the hole in the leafy canopy overhead. This solid canopy is vital to the well-being of the forest. Raindrops shatter into a kind of mist when they strike the canopy. By blocking most direct sunlight, the tree-fern canopy also helps maintain a constant moist, cool microclimate—home for a special plant-animal community. Pigs disrupt this community by killing fallen tree ferns, allowing raindrops and sunlight to reach the forest floor.

The Hawaiian rain forest includes tall ohia lehua trees and tree ferns. Feral pigs harm the tree ferns and alter the microclimate of the forest floor.

According to park biologist Daniel Taylor, the pigs' taste for tree ferns causes further harm. He explained, "The eaten cores of tree-fern trunks form troughs in which rainwater collects. This water becomes a breeding place for mosquitoes. Mosquitoes are not native here, nor is the avian [bird] malaria that they carry. The native bird population doesn't tolerate the malaria very well. . . . We think one of the major causes, if not *the* major cause, of the decline of native forest birds is avian malaria."

The park service hopes to eliminate feral pigs from the Hawaii Volcanoes National Park—no easy task. Feral pigs are fast and agile. They dash through brushy tangles that a human must chop through. State biologists who studied wild pigs on the island of Hawaii reported, "The terrain of some of Hawaii's forests is almost unbelievable: deep, steep-wall canyons, dense tangles of staghorn fern, knee-deep mud, water-slick rocks; all of this the wild pigs penetrate easily and by choice."

In its war against feral pigs, the park service uses tactics that were successful against feral goats. A population of fifteen thousand goats in 1970 was reduced to two hundred by 1985. The tactics: fences around the park boundary, fences between different areas within the park, and intensive, well-organized hunting and tracking. Six full-time hunters, aided by dogs, have already reduced the feral-pig population significantly.

There is little hope that all exotic animals and plants will ever be removed from the forests of this national park, but the eradication of goats and pigs is within reach. Their removal will bring the forests a step closer to wholeness.

CHAPTER FIVE

Rivers and Lakes

"You cannot step twice in the same river, for fresh waters are ever flowing upon you."

Heraclitus
Fragments of Heraclitus

Water in motion is the essence of rivers and other streams. A river's water is constantly renewed from upstream tributaries and from the groundwater of its basin. Rivers have a tremendous capacity to renew themselves, to recover from chemical spills, sewage outflows, and other ecological insults. Given a chance, a river can restore itself. Recovery can take decades, however, when toxic substances rest in sediments, when a river's banks have been stripped of their natural vegetation, or when a river has been forced into an unnaturally straight path.

In the United States, many thousands of miles of rivers have been straightened, or channelized, by the Army Corps of Engineers and by the Soil Conservation Service. Channelization involves straightening a stream or dredging a new channel to which water is diverted. Tree- and shrub-lined streams with curving and even meandering channels are changed into sluiceways with barren banks. The goal is to move water downstream quickly and reduce local flooding, allowing agricultural or other use of the flood plain.

Channelization often accomplishes its goal, but at great cost. Water rushes down the ditch to inundate areas farther downstream. Increased water velocity erodes stream banks.

After a section of Missouri's Blackwater River was channelized, the riverbed grew wider and wider. Most bridges had to be replaced or lengthened several times. One riverbed that was originally 25 yards across now measures 136 yards.

Fish populations in channelized parts of the Blackwater were found to be only one fifth of those in natural stretches of the river. Channelization removes woody vegetation from riverbanks and thereby eliminates cooling shade for fish in the summer. Also, any features that would slow water flow are removed. With them go wildlife and natural beauty.

One of the most destructive channelization projects took place in central Florida. Its victim was the Kissimmee River, which arises from lakes and used to meander south to Lake Okeechobee. The Kissimmee and its floodplain were rich in fish, water birds, and other wildlife. Trouble began in 1947, when hurricanes and unusual amounts of rain caused flooding in the southern half of Florida. The state asked the Army Corps of Engineers for help.

Part of the corps' solution was to change the meandering 98-mile-long Kissimmee into a 52-mile-long, 200-foot-wide canal through which water would flow quickly to Lake Okeechobee and then to the Atlantic Ocean. Work was completed by 1970, and the folly of channelizing the Kissimmee was soon apparent. Fish and aquatic plants began dying in Lake Okeechobee—a result of the destruction of marshes along the Kissimmee. Forty thousand acres of marshes had once served as a filter for water reaching Lake Okeechobee. Now that natural filter was mostly gone, replaced by farmland that contributed cow manure, fertilizer, and eroded soil to the water entering the lake. Diversion of water from Lake Okeechobee to the ocean also reduced underground water supplies south of the lake, allowing salt water to intrude, harming agriculture and the Everglades National Park.

Before channelization, waters of the Kissimmee River were filtered through marshes along its meandering course.

As early as 1971, a report issued at the Governor's Conference on Water Management in South Florida called for reflooding the Kissimmee River marshes. In 1978 the state of Florida asked the Corps of Engineers to reevaluate the project and to prepare a plan for restoring the Kissimmee. In 1983 the state lost patience with the corps and devised its own plan for restoring the river. Ironically, the Kissimmee is a navigable river and therefore is under the jurisdiction of the Corps of Engineers, so the state needs the corps' approval in order to undo the corps' own work.

The South Florida Water Management District sought permission to fill in parts of the Kissimmee canal, to divert water into parts of the former river channel, and to reflood some former marshes. The corps refused. Although it had spent 30 million dollars in public money to channelize the Kissimmee, it claimed that such funds cannot be used to restore a river. However, a compromise was arranged for part of the work (paid for by Florida). By 1986 water was being diverted into about 13 miles of old river channel and adjacent marshlands.

In the next stage of proposed restoration, parts of the canal would be filled in. This is still resisted by the Corps of Engineers. Although there are many political and financial obstacles to be overcome, state water managers and leaders of environmental groups envision a time when the Kissimmee River will once again flow slowly through much of its old channel, filter water through riverside marshes, support abundant fish and wildlife, and help improve the water supply of southern Florida.

The Kissimmee River and its adjoining marshes will not need to be restocked with fish, aquatic insects, and aquatic plants. Once conditions are favorable, these organisms usually disperse through water and restock populations in flowing water ecosystems. But people can speed the process, as they did in the restoration of the Quashnet River on southwestern Cape Cod in Massachusetts.In his book *Restoring the Earth,* author John Berger gives a detailed account of the Quashnet restoration.

Once a fine trout stream, the Quashnet meandered clear and cold through tall forests. Then the forests were cleared and the river was dammed for a gristmill's energy supply. Later, about 1895, the river basin was ditched and diked into cranberry bogs. After the bogs were abandoned the river became a broad, brush-choked stream, which John Berger described as "a jungle so overgrown that fishermen could scarcely find the river anymore, much less fish it."

Today the Quashnet is dramatically different, thanks to thousands of hours of labor by members of the Southeastern Massachusetts and Cape Cod Chapters of Trout Unlimited. Beginning in the summer of 1976, volunteers cut brush and built stream-flow deflectors, silt control devices, and streambank trout shelters. They planted native trees to stabilize banks, help cool the water, and prevent the growth of shrubs.

Few aquatic insects were found in the Quashnet when the restoration project began; pesticides used by cranberry growers had wiped out many species. Project workers collected insect nymphs, crayfish, and other invertebrates from a healthier river and let them go in the Quashnet. In 1983 there was evidence that another part of the river's life had been restored—mayflies were seen hatching from its waters. Eventually, sea-run brook trout will be stocked in the river, reintroduced to waters from which they had been missing for one hundred fifty years. In one decade the little Quashnet was changed from a mostly straight, slow, shallow, brush-choked stream to a curving, fast, deep, open river, well on its way to resembling the rich ecosystem that existed in pre-Colonial times.

As difficult as the Quashnet restoration was, it was helped by a powerful ally—flowing water—that is not available in lakes. Although lake water is replaced, its rate of change is measured in months, years, and sometimes decades. California's Lake Tahoe is so deep that seven hundred years are needed for complete renewal of its water.

Lakes are sinks that trap sediments and gradually become marshes, then dry land. As nutrients flow into a lake and accumulate in its sediments, they stimulate growth of plant and animal life. Nutrient-rich lakes are highly productive but eventually become oxygen-poor, choked with decaying algae and other vegetation. This natural aging process is called eutrophication.

Humans hasten eutrophication by increasing the inputs of nutrients from sewage-treatment plants, septic-tank drainage, fertilizer runoff from fields and lawns, and storm-water runoff. Thousands of North American lakes and ponds show symptoms of accelerated eutrophication. In extreme cases these include dense growths and surface scums of blue-green algae and fish dead from lack of oxygen. The more eutrophic a lake, the less recreation it offers and the lower the quality of its drinking water.

Phosphorus is the key nutrient. Its absence restrains the growth of algae and other microorganisms; its abundance promotes their growth. An overabundance of phosphorus hastens eutrophication. The most basic step in lake restoration is to first reduce the inflow of phosphorus and, to a lesser extent, nitrogen. Phosphates were once common ingredients of laundry detergents and contributed as much as 60 percent of the

Members of Trout Unlimited built stream flow deflectors, cleared brush, planted native trees, and even stocked aquatic insects in their effort to restore the Quashnet River.

phosphorus in municipal sewage. Most of this phosphorus remained in water released from sewage treatment plants. Introduction of low-phosphate detergents helped slow eutrophication of countless lakes. The most advanced sewage treatment plants today also help limit eutrophication. They can remove as much as 98 percent of phosphorus from sewage. Completion of many of these plants in cities near the Great Lakes has cut phosphorus input by three fourths or more and improved lake water quality.

Florida's Lake Okeechobee, second largest lake by surface area in the United States, is eutrophic, with 20 percent of its phorphorus carried in by the waters of the channelized Kissimmee River. In 1986 more than a hundred square miles of its surface was covered with blue-green algae—an alarming sign of eutrophication and declining water quality. Since the lake is the major surface reservoir of south-central Florida, water managers are working to reduce runoff of nutrients from livestock pastures and feedlots, and from fertilized land where vegetables and sugarcane are grown.

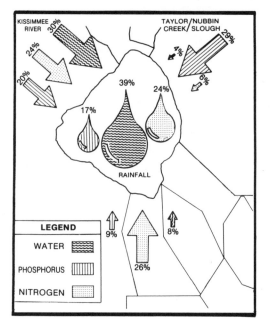

This drawing shows the sources of water and nutrients that enter Lake Okeechobee. The lake will become increasingly more eutrophic unless the inflow of phosphorus and nitrogen is reduced.

At Lake Minnetonka in Minnesota, the major source of phosphorus was storm-water runoff, which carries fertilizers from fields and lawns. The storm waters were diverted through a marshy area before entering the lake, and the wetland now retains 78 percent of all phosphorus and 94 percent of suspended solids from the storm water. The wetland and its wildlife continue to thrive, while less algae grows in Lake Minnetonka. A similar wetland phosphorus-filter was set up at Clear Lake, near Waseca, Minnesota. Clear Lake had become progressively less clear with recurring algae blooms, but it improved once the inflow of phosphorus was reduced.

In many cases, a reduction of phorphorus input does not improve water quality much. The lake is already overloaded with nutrients dissolved in water and stored in vegetation and sediments. Here lies the greatest challenge of lake restoration: to remove nutrients already present.

Excessive nutrients in a few lakes can be reduced by increasing the rate at which their water is replaced. Green Lake in Seattle, Washington, receives nutrients from storm-water runoff. Low-phosphorus water from the city water supply was added so that the lake's volume of water was replaced about three times a year. This cut the lake's load of nutrients in half.

The water quality of some small lakes has been somewhat improved by actually dredging sediments from the lake bottom. Dredging is the most costly method of nutrient removal. Chemical treatments are more economical. Chemicals were first used in 1962 to reduce nutrient concentrations of lakes in the Netherlands and have since been used in many North American lakes.

Certain chemical agents combine with phosphorus to form insoluble compounds that settle to the lake bottom. Often the material on the bottom blocks further release of phosphorus from sediments. In 1977 this treatment was tried in 156-acre Medical Lake in Washington State. Two scientists treated the lake with 1,030 tons of alum (aluminum sulfate), applying it from a homemade barge. Alum was spread four times on the surface and injected seven times into deep water.

The results were dramatic, with more than 80 percent of the lake's phosphorus removed and algae populations cut by more than 90 percent. Similar results have been obtained at lakes in Wisconsin and Ohio, and have lasted for as long as six years. Figuring the correct dose of alum for a lake is critical. Too little alum will fail to attract the phosphorus; too much may add toxic amounts of soluble aluminum to the water. Lakes vary so in their water chemistry, water replacement rate, sources of nutrients, and other features that there is no easy formula for treating eutrophication.

Chemical treatment can also temporarily restore lakes whose waters are becoming too acidic for living things—the result of acid rain. Actually, acid deposition is a more accurate name than acid rain. The burning of coal, oil, and natural gas releases sulfur dioxide and nitrogen oxides that can be carried aloft for hundreds of miles and fall to earth with rain, snow, and fog—or as acidic particles on dry, clear days.

Eastern Canada and northeastern United States have been hard hit by acid rain, with several thousand lakes and ponds so acidified that they support little or no life. In Sweden and Norway, acid rain has been a matter of concern since the 1960s. Sweden has the world's largest chemical treatment program, applying lime to acidified lakes and streams. Lime is a base, or alkaline compound, the chemical opposite of an acid, and neutralizes incoming acids in water. By 1986, lime had been applied to twenty thousand bodies of water in Sweden. New York State has the largest liming program in the United States. The cost varies from about fifty dollars per acre for lakes with easy access by boat to several hundred dollars an acre for remote lakes limed from a helicopter.

The liming of acidified lakes is no cure for acid rain and its effects. It is a short-term, temporary measure to protect aquatic life or to allow its restoration to a lake. Liming does

Workers spread powdered limestone, delivered by helicopter, on the frozen surface of a lake in northern New York. When the ice melts, the limestone temporarily counteracts the harmful effects of acidic air pollutants.

nothing to reduce the daily dose of acidic compounds from the atmosphere. Only stopping pollutants at their source will do that.

Acidified or eutrophic lakes are especially frustrating problems because the sources of pollutants may be far away and politically difficult to affect. Some lakes have more tangible problems that seem simple by comparison. One such lake is Sweden's Lake Hornborga. Early in the twentieth century it covered 18 square miles with a maximum depth of 10 feet. It was a popular fishing lake and one of the most famous waterfowl lakes in northwestern Europe.

Then the Swedish government began to lower lake levels to obtain more farmland. By the 1930s, most of Lake Hornborga was dry in summer. It would probably still be dry but its bottom soils proved to be poor for farming and were abandoned. By 1968 more than 7 square miles of the former lake were covered with a monoculture of the common reed *Phragmites communis*. Also called foxtail reed, *Phragmites* has attractive plumelike seed heads—perhaps its only virtue. It is an aggressive weed with little food value for wildlife. Ecologists consider *Phragmites* a symptom of a degraded aquatic habitat, an apt description of mostly drained Lake Hornborga.

The Swedish government funded research to see whether Lake Hornborga could be restored. Ecologists soon recognized that simply raising the water level would not do.

Thick stands of *Phragmites*, the common reed, form a wetland monoculture that reduces the variety of plant and animal life.

Phragmites had laid down a thick layer of dead leaves and stems. Below that lay interwoven root systems in the mud. This mass of bottom detritus would decay under water and deplete oxygen supplies. It was also a poor surface for development of the native invertebrate populations and submerged plants still found in the open-water remnant of Lake Hornborga.

Swedish scientists and engineers devised ways to rid the basin of *Phragmites*. Mowing machines moved over ice in winter, clipping off the stems, which were burned. During the spring high-water period, mowing machines on pontoon wheels cut the reed stubble under water and also ripped up the bottom detritus. Most of it washed ashore and was burned in the summer. Amphibious machines cut the green shoots in summer and also rototilled the mud.

Cleared of *Phragmites,* shallow-water areas were soon colonized by native aquatic flora and fauna. Ducks and geese began to rediscover Lake Hornborga, which was restored to its approximate former 10-foot depth. One large lake, once largely degraded to the state of a weed monoculture, has been restored to its full richness, complexity, and beauty.

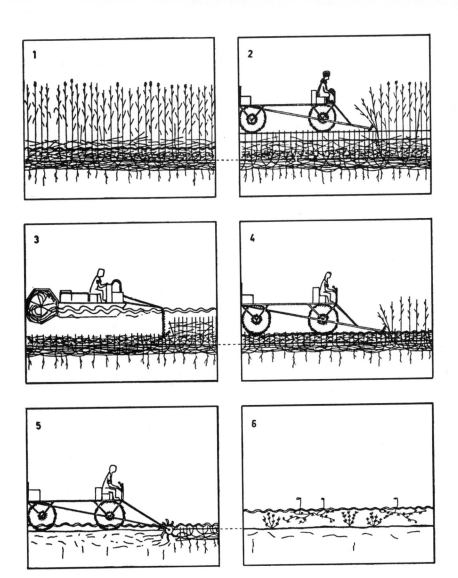

To restore the mostly-drained Lake Hornborga, Swedish ecologists attacked more than 7 square miles of *Phragmites*. The reeds arose from a dense layer of roots, dead leaves and stems (1). In the wintertime, machines mowed down all stems above the ice (2), and the stems were burned. During the spring high-water period, machines cut reed stems and ripped up layers of dead stems (3). In the summer low-water period, machines mowed new reed shoots (4) and rototilled the lake mud (5). Once rid of the dense stands of reeds, the lake supported native aquatic plants when its original water level was restored (6).

CHAPTER SIX

The Greatest Challenge

"We abuse the land because we regard it as a commodity belonging to us. When we see the land as a community to which we belong, we may begin to use it with love and respect."

Aldo Leopold
A Sand County Almanac

"Moonscape" and "a landing place for extraterrestrials" are terms sometimes used to describe lands that have been strip-mined. They are among the most damaged lands on earth. Yet they can be reclaimed to usefulness; sometimes they can even be restored to their original condition. However, lands like these give restorationists their greatest challenge.

Huge power shovels and other modern earth-moving equipment enable us to strip away a hundred feet or more of soil and rock to reach deposits of fuels and minerals. Besides coal, other strip-mined fuels are uranium, oil shale, and tar sands. Surface-mined minerals include iron, phosphates, manganese, copper, mica, kaolin (china clay), gravel, and sand.

Layers of soils and rocks are stripped away in order to reach deposits of coal, other fuels, or minerals.

In the United States about 6 million acres of land have been strip-mined in twenty-seven states—an area about the size of New Hampshire. Very little has been reclaimed or restored. In contrast, it is difficult to see evidence of past surface-mining in England and West Germany. There, the land is reshaped after mining, the subsoil and topsoil replaced, and the area returned to productive use. For the most part, however, surface-mined lands abroad and in the United States are reclaimed, not restored.

For decades, U.S. surface-mine operators were not required to reclaim or restore their work sites. The results were—and still are—disastrous, especially in the Appalachians, where coal seams often lie half to two thirds of the way up mountainsides. Whole mountaintops were scalped of their vegetation and soil, or mountain slopes were gouged out to build temporary roads in order to reach coal. Following the contour of the coal seam along the slope, miners made deep, shelflike cuts, creating an almost vertical wall and pushing trees and soil downhill. Landslides were common on these unstable slopes, and soil eroded into rivers and streams. On more level terrain, a completed coal strip-mining operation resembled a large-scale ploughed field of ridges and furrows, called ridge-ravine topography.

Strip miners followed the contour of coal seams, gouged out mountainsides, dumped trees and soils downhill, then moved on.

Whether in mountains or plains, surface mining often brings iron pyrite (iron disulfide) to the surface. Exposing this compound to the air produces iron and sulfuric acid. The acid leaches aluminum, copper, manganese, and zinc from rocks. These metals combined with acids drain from the mine into streams. Nationwide, acid mine drainage has wiped out aquatic life from thousands of miles of streams.

Until the 1960s, when some states began to require reclamation, strip miners just took the coal they wanted and moved on. Then a natural healing process began, with plants invading and taking root wherever they could. Recovery was often agonizingly slow.

The topsoil was usually buried by a compacted jumble of subsoil and rocks that was usually low in nutrients needed for plant growth. The soil chemistry, its ability to retain water, and other vital characteristics varied widely over the disturbed surface. A scientist who studied an Ohio strip mine found some areas still unable to support much plant life fifty-seven years after the mine was abandoned. Another study of seventy-to one-hundred-thirty-year-old surface-mine soils showed that natural soils were still superior in several important features, including soil porosity and amounts of nitrogen and organic matter.

In the 1960s state after state began to demand some reclamation by strip mine operators. In 1977, after a decade of resistance from the coal industry, a federal bill requiring reclamation was signed into law by President Jimmy Carter. Although enforcement is weak and mine operators in some states exploit loopholes in the law, the Surface Mining Control and Reclamation Act has led to reclamation of many new surface coal mine operations and also of some older, abandoned sites. The law has also stimulated research in reclamation methods and the possibility of actually restoring ecosystems degraded by strip-mining.

To be most effective and economical, reclamation must be planned before mining begins. Information about water drainage is critical. Samples of soils and underlying rocks can be analyzed to get some idea of their chemistry. Then, as the soils and rocks are removed, they can be piled so that more fertile and less acid-producing materials are the last layers to be spread over the site.

Usually the original topsoil is the final layer, but there are exceptions to this procedure. In some regions, below-ground deposits have greater fertility and potential for plant growth than the topsoil. In one Australian strip mine, for example, the original soils were poor in nutrients. Shale rock dug up in mining broke down quickly into an excellent soil that supported a lush grassland. This was a particularly successful reclamation; it was *not* restoration, since the goals of ecological restoration are to recreate a natural community, even one with rather infertile soils.

Burying iron pyrite is a vital step in reclamation that reduces or eliminates acid drainage. Mine operators often build diversion ditches or special ponds in which to trap sediments. Steep-sided slopes are graded into gentle slopes to reduce erosion. After soils are rearranged on the land they can be fertilized and seeded or planted. Simply scattering seeds often

Strip-mined lands can be reclaimed with plantings of shrubs and trees, and applications of mulch and fertilizers.

fails; covering them with soil greatly improves their chances of survival and germination. A mulch of straw may be needed to prevent erosion until plants are well established. Additional fertilizer may be needed from time to time.

In the Appalachians, getting a grassy cover on the soil is especially important because abundant rain threatens erosion of the hilly terrain. In 1983 David Samuel, a West Virginia wildlife biologist, reported that more than 100,000 acres of grasslands had been created on surface-mine sites in West Virginia alone. The ground cover stabilized the soil and also provided a habitat for large populations of mice, but discouraged some other kinds of native wildlife. This is reclamation, not restoration, and large grasslands are not typical of the region. Native grassland sparrows and horned larks had difficulty finding nest sites in the dense growth of these new prairies. Bobwhite quail and wild turkeys had difficulty feeding there. Samuel and other biologists recommended periodic burning of the mine grasslands and increased planting of trees and shrubs to improve these habitats for wildlife.

Reclamation of some mine sites in the Appalachians has produced broad grasslands where none occur naturally.

Reclamation regulations call for returning the land to its approximate original contours. In some situations, however, landscape changes wrought by mining are an improvement over what existed before. In Florida, for example, phosphate mining leaves settling ponds scattered through the forest. Filling them with soil and restoring the entire area to woodland would be very costly. It would also eliminate a pond-forest mixture that is more diverse and attractive to birds and other wildlife than forest alone.

The basic goals of mine reclamation are to prevent acid drainage and erosion, and to cover the soil with some plants—*not* to restore native vegetation and plant-animal communities. Of the nearly two hundred kinds of grasses, forbs, shrubs, and trees sometimes planted on surface-mine sites, many are exotic species from other continents. There is, however, a trend toward using and encouraging native plants.

Wisconsin's mine reclamation law has a specific goal of restoring native plants. It has been applied to the huge amounts of tailings (wastes) produced where taconite is processed into iron ore. After they are fertilized and mulched, the tailings support the growth of several prairie plants that are native to the area. In the alpine ecosystems of western mountains, native plants are known to be superior to the commonly available exotic species when ecologists try to heal damage caused by mining, mineral exploration, or access roads.

Native plants have also been used successfully on surface-mine sites in arid or semiarid regions. Under the best of circumstances, plants are hard to establish in desert areas with their sparse rainfall and thin, poor topsoils. Plant ecologists in Arizona have discovered that mycorrhizal fungi in the soil are vital for the survival of nearly all of the dominant native shrubs of the Southwest. For example, the four-wing saltbush,

A Virginia strip mine (top photo) was planted with seedlings of coniferous trees, which began to cover the area after 3 years (middle photo) and 8 years (bottom photo). This is reclamation, not the more challenging restoration of a natural forest on the land.

a shrub commonly planted on strip-mined soils, grows much better when provided with mycorrhizae than without. The scientists are investigating ways to inoculate mycorrhizal fungi into the soils of restored mine sites.

At the Navaho Coal Mine in northwestern New Mexico, native desert plants are used by Utah International, the mine operator, to revegetate the land. Bill Skeet, an agricultural engineer, directs the work, planting seeds of fifteen native grasses, forbs, and shrubs. The land surface is mulched with straw and irrigated for a year on a schedule that follows the natural rainfall pattern of the area. This gets the seedlings off to a good start. Then the plants are on their own, although they are protected from grazing. Rainfall is just five to six inches a year.

Four-wing saltbush, Indian rice grass, and other native plants survive, but the vegetation looks as sparse as that on nearby land that has been overgrazed for decades. Ecologists cannot say with certainty what the natural vegetation was like a century ago. However, Bill Skeet has been told by old-time residents that native grasses grew "belly high" in parts of the region before overgrazing took its toll.

Utah International is not required to restore the land to that long-ago condition. By law a mining company need only bring the land back to the state that existed just before mining began. In much of the arid West, that is already a badly overgrazed, impoverished environment, a far cry from what it once was and could again be.

Restorationists are tempted to bring back those "belly high" grasses, to truly heal the land. Part of their motivation is curiosity about the mysteries of nature. William R. Jordan, III, editor of *Restoration & Management Notes,* explained, "The restorationist, like the artist, will find himself or herself looking at nature in new and more critical ways, for it is not the taking apart but the attempt to put together that provokes the most stringent tests of perception and understanding."

Although restoration projects are usually planned and managed by botanists, ecologists, or other trained professionals, many restorations succeed only because of the volunteer efforts of ordinary people, both young and old. Those interested in becoming involved in this field may find a nearby project by inquiring at nature centers, arboretums, botanical gardens, zoos, or at the botany or natural resources departments of local colleges. Also, *Research & Management Notes* (see Further Reading, p. 60) reports on projects all over North America.

Restorationists feel that their work is vitally important for humanity. They recognize the value of natural places as havens for endangered plants and animals and as storehouses for the earth's genetic diversity. They also feel they are part of the land. By healing some of the scars humans have inflicted on nature, they restore themselves.

acid rain (acid deposition)—a process in which gases of sulfur and nitrogen are released into the air, where portions of them are converted to acids that fall to the ground in rain, snow, or as dry deposits. The gases are given off during combustion of coal, gasoline, and other fossil fuels.

arboretum—an area set aside for the cultivation of woody plants (trees and shrubs) for educational and scientific purposes.

Civilian Conservation Corps (CCC)—an agency of the federal government created to provide work for unemployed young men. Between 1933 and 1942, nearly 3 million men planted trees and worked on other conservation projects for the CCC.

community—in an ecological sense, all of the plants and animals in a particular environment.

ecological restoration—". . . an effort to imitate nature in all its artistry and complexity by taking a degraded system and making it more diverse and productive. . . ." John Berger.

ecology—the study of the relationships between living things and their environment.

ecosystem—all of the living and nonliving parts of a given area in nature. Ecosystems range in size from puddles to oceans.

environment—all of the surroundings of an organism, including other living things, climate, and soils.

eutrophication—the process by which a body of water becomes enriched with minerals and other nutrients.

habitat—the living place or immediate surroundings of an organism.

microclimate—the climate in the immediate vicinity of an organism or object. It is the climate that is really significant for the comfort and survival of an organism.

minimum critical size—the smallest area of habitat needed for a population of an animal or plant species to sustain itself.

monoculture—growth of a single plant species that dominates an environment. Monocultures are usually human-made, for example, a field planted with a single variety of wheat, a forest planted with a single tree species.

mycorrhizae—fungi that live on or within the roots or rhizomes of many plants and which absorb nutrients from the soil that are used by the plants.

nutrient—a substance needed for normal growth and development of an organism.

reclamation—the process of making something more useful or productive, for example, making strip-mined land suitable for farming.

restoration ecology—restoration of environments carried out specifically as a technique for raising questions and testing ideas about ecology.

restorationist—a person who seeks to restore a damaged environment to a more natural condition, with as much as possible of its native plant-animal community.

Further Reading

The best single source of information about restoration projects all over North America is the journal *Restoration & Management Notes,* published twice a year by the University of Wisconsin Press. You can find current and past issues in the libraries of botanical gardens, science museums, and universities.

Belous, Robert. "Restoration Among the Redwoods." *Restoration & Management Notes,* Vol. 2, Number 2 (Winter 1984), pp. 57-65.

Berger, John. *Restoring the Earth: How Americans are Working to Renew Our Damaged Environment.* New York: Alfred A. Knopf, 1985.

Bradshaw, A.D., and M.J. Chadwick. *The Restoration of Land.* Berkeley: University of California Press, 1980.

Branson, Branley. "Is There Life After Strip Mining?" *Natural History* (August 1986), pp. 31-37.

Brower, Kenneth. "The Pig War." *The Atlantic Monthly* (August 1985), pp. 44-58.

Cairns, John Jr., K. Dickson, and E. Herricks. *Recovery and Restoration of Damaged Ecosystems.* Charlottesville: University of Virginia Press, 1977.

Cox, Thomas, et al. *This Well-Wooded Land: Americans and Their Forests from Colonial Times to the Present.* Lincoln: University of Nebraska Press, 1985.

Cullimore, Duke. "Restoration of a River." *Sierra* (September-October 1985), pp. 18-23.

Gore, James, editor. *The Restoration of Rivers and Streams.* Boston: Butterworths, 1985.

Jordan, William III. "Hint of Green." *Restoration & Management Notes,* Vol. 1, Number 4 (summer 1983), pp. 4-10.

———. Michael Gilpin, and J.D. Aber, editors. *Restoration Ecology: A Synthetic Approach to Ecological Research.* New York: Cambridge University Press, 1987.

———. "Working With the River." *Restoration & Management Notes,* Vol. 2, Number 1 (summer 1984), pp. 4-11.

Josselyn, Michael, editor. *Wetland Restoration and Enhancement in California.* A California Sea Grant College Program Publication, Tiburon Center for Environment Studies Technical Report Number 2 (December 1982).

Laycock, George. "A Scourge of Goats." *Audubon* (April 1984), pp. 100-103.

Leopold, Aldo. *A Sand County Almanac.* New York: Oxford University Press, 1966.

Maugh, Thomas II. "Restoring Damaged Lakes." *Science* (February 2, 1979), pp. 425-427.

Miller, R. Michael. "Mycorrhizae." *Restoration & Management Notes,* Vol. 3, Number 1 (summer 1985), pp. 14-20.

Pringle, Laurence. *Estuaries: Where Rivers Meet the Sea.* New York: Macmillan, 1973.

———. *Feral: Tame Animals Gone Wild.* New York: Macmillan, 1983.

———. *Natural Fire: Its Ecology in Forests.* New York: Wm. Morrow and Company, 1979.

———. *What Shall We Do With the Land?* New York: T. Y. Crowell, 1981.

Taggert, Judith, editor. *Lake Restoration, Protection, and Management.* Proceedings of the Second Annual Conference of the North American Lake Management Society. Washington, D.C.: Environmental Protection Agency, 1982.

Temple, Truman. "The Marsh Maker of St. Michaels." *The Amicus Journal* (Summer 1983), pp. 33-37.

Teal, John and Mildred. *Life and Death of the Salt Marsh.* New York: Ballantine Books, 1969.

Vogel, Willis. *A Guide for Revegetating Coal Minesoils in the Eastern United States.* General Technical Report NE-68, Northeastern Forest Experiment Station, U.S. Department of Agriculture, 1981.

Vogl, Richard. "Fire: A Destructive Menace or a Natural Process?" In Cairns, et al, *Recovery and Restoration of Damaged Ecosystems.* Charlottesville: University of Virginia Press, 1977.

Index